D1299873

THE MYSTERIOUS CASE OF
SIR ARTHUR CONAN DOYLE

World Writers

THE MYSTERIOUS CASE OF SIR ARTHUR CONAN DOYLE

Cynthia Adams

620 South Elm Street, Suite 223
Greensboro, NC 27406 USA

The Mysterious Case of Sir Arthur Conan Doyle

Copyright © 1999 by Cynthia Adams

Library of Congress Cataloging-in-Publication Data
Adams, Cynthia, 1953
   The mysterious case of Sir Arthur Conan Doyle / Cynthia Adams. — 1st ed.
      p. cm. — (World writers)
   Includes bibliographical references and index.
   Summary: Discusses the life and work of Sir Arthur Conan Doyle and his famous
creation, Sherlock Holmes.
      ISBN   1-883846-34-X
            1. Doyle, Arthur Conan, Sir, 1859-1930 —Juvenile literature. 2. Authors,
Scottish—19th century—Biography—Juvenile literature. 3. Holmes, Sherlock (Fictitious
character)—Juvenile literature. [1. Doyle, Arthur Conan, Sir, 1859-1930.   2. Authors,
Scottish. 3. Holmes, Sherlock (Fictitious character)]   I. Title   II. Series.
PR4623.A15   1999
823' .8—dc21
[B]

                                                                    99-11668
                                                                       CIP

Printed in the United States of America
First Edition

To Don

Contents

Sir Arthur Conan Doyle

Chapter One

A Storyteller in Training

Conan Doyle wrote his first book when he was six. It was an adventure story, and he drew the illustrations himself. He thought later that the little book "showed the set of his mind." Conan was captivated by mystery, adventure, and the world of the imagination. It was so much more exciting than the dull streets of Edinburgh, Scotland, in the 1860s. He believed he could create his own reality. Maybe he was right. Years later his imagination led him to create Sherlock Holmes, one of the most intriguing characters in all of literature.

For more than a century, audiences the world over have been mesmerized by the brilliant detective. Readers are captivated by this scientist of crime who smokes a pipe and wears a deerstalker hat as he travels the foggy streets of nineteenth century London. They love following his exploits as he uses his keen powers of observation to solve baffling mysteries.

In Doyle's own time, readers followed Holmes' adventures through stories published each month in popular magazines. Today, his stories are published in books. There are millions of copies printed in dozens of languages. There have been more than sixty movies and television dramas about the famous detective. Holmes' fictional study at 221B Baker Street in London has been turned into a real-life museum honoring his memory. Fan clubs around the world celebrate Holmes, with members often dressing up in nineteenth century costumes to commemorate the detective's legend. The attraction of the genius of Baker Street is so powerful that many of his fans insist that he actually lived—and that Arthur Conan Doyle is the made up character!

Seldom has a fictional character come so alive for so many readers. Any writer should be proud to have created such a memorable figure of world literature. Why then did Conan Doyle, after only a few months of writing the stories, grow to hate Sherlock Holmes—to the point of even killing him off midway through his career? What prompted him to create this famous detective in the first place? How did he go about doing it? The logical way to start answering these questions is by beginning with the childhood of the boy who longed to imagine his own reality.

Mary Doyle, Conan's mother (he called her The Ma'am), loved to tell stories. His earliest memory, a couple of years after his birth in 1859, was of him huddling by the fire for warmth and listening as his mother told him a story while tending to his baby sister Connie.

Sometimes she told horror stories in a voice so full of fear that goose bumps rose over Conan's arms. The fire popped

This drawing of four-year-old Conan Doyle was made by his Uncle Richard.

and crackled as he'd wait, breath held, for the next twist of the plot. Once, The Ma'am became so involved in a story she was telling that she stuck the porridge spoon in the baby's ear instead of her mouth. Sometimes The Ma'am told stories in the French she'd studied as a student. There was usually a white knight, chivalrous and good, who saved the day in her stories. Mary Doyle also loved languages, literature, and anything to do with history.

When The Ma'am's lively stories ended, there was only the sound of the crackling fire or the scratching of Conan's father's pencil against paper. Charles Doyle was an artist, from a family of artists. He loved to draw eerie images. The ghosts, specters, and the wild and fearsome scenes he drew could make Conan shudder as much as his mother's stories. Charles Doyle spent most of his time alone in the corner. He seemed to not notice what went on around him as he bent over his drawing pad.

The Doyles were Irish Catholics who had immigrated to Edinburgh from Ireland. Though Charles was artistic, he never became successful. He worked as a low-paid government clerk. His small income allowed the family to barely scrape by. Sometimes the family took in boarders to make ends meet. During the hardest times, they moved to smaller quarters. All of this, Conan said, made him more resilient and persistent.

Charles Doyle also suffered from epilepsy, something the family kept secret. Little was known about the causes or treatment of the disorder. Doctors could only treat the

Doyle's mother spent hours telling him stories of knights and other heroes.

symptoms with narcotics and Charles became addicted to the powerful drugs prescribed for his condition. Conan struggled to understand his father's condition as he watched him use needles and strange medicines. Compared to his vivacious mother, his father was a brooder and a mystery. He was often withdrawn and kept to himself. This was confusing to the boy. Conan respected and feared his father at the same time, and despite his health problems, Conan considered him to be a gentleman.

Conan lived with his family in a one-level apartment in a crowded, working-class neighborhood. The poorer families lived in the single-level flats. The more well-to-do lived in villas, opposite where Conan lived. Ten children were born into the Doyle family, and seven survived.

The streets of Edinburgh were rough. The kids who lived in the flats resented and fought with the villa kids. Conan loved the combat. "We lived in the hardy and bracing atmosphere of poverty," Conan wrote later, "and each in turn did our best to help those who were younger than ourselves."

One afternoon after school, Conan fought an older boy, Eddie Tulloch, the son of a bootmaker. Eddie knocked him to the ground with a cloth bag full of books. The bag struck Conan's head with such force he almost passed out. He lay senseless a few minutes before heading home with his blackened eye.

He felt humiliated, and decided that it was the last time he would submit to abuse or to life's unfairness. He wanted

Charles Doyle was ill during most of Conan's childhood.

to fight back, not shrink away as his father had. Conan also learned how he wanted to live his life from The Ma'am's noble stories about white knights and courageous deeds.

Later, when he saw a bully pick on an old man, Conan raced over to help him. The bully turned on him and made sure Conan paid the price for his gallantry. But he didn't mind. He needed courage to live his life. Good and evil, and how people lived their lives, fascinated him.

Conan grew big and strong. His wrists and ankles jutted out of his clothes. He felt pleased by his size and growth. Eddie Tulloch may have given him a black eye, but it wasn't long before he was large enough to get his revenge.

The most intimidating bully of all was one he couldn't even fight. At his Edinburgh school he had to contend with a mean-spirited, one-eyed schoolmaster. The teacher's face was marked with scars. He terrified Conan. The teacher made his days miserable with punishments, beatings and criticism.

"Of my boyhood," Conan said years later, "I could say little, save that it was Spartan at home and more Spartan at the Edinburgh school."

Conan was excited when it came time to leave Edinburgh school for a more advanced education. He was sure that any new school would be better than the one dominated by the one-eyed schoolmaster.

Chapter Two

Young Writer's Beginnings

In the Scotland of a hundred years ago, any boy who wanted a proper education had to go away from home to boarding school. Often it was a hard life. The buildings were drafty, teachers were often cruel, and the boys were separated from their families for months at a time.

Because Conan was his family's eldest son, they pinned their highest hopes on him. Conan needed a proper education, and his uncle Michael, Conan's godfather, was determined to see that he got it.

Michael, who worked in Paris as the editor of a French art magazine, liked his young nephew. Conan had sometimes sent his uncle little stories or verses he had written. Conan told him about his favorite books, *Ivanhoe*, by Sir Walter Scott and *Scalp Hunter* by the Irish writer Mayne Reid. Michael often mailed Conan some books and occasional gifts of money. Conan usually bought books with the money.

Two other uncles, both well-to-do, also helped pay for Conan's schooling. Uncle Henry Doyle was the manager of the National Gallery at Dublin. Richard was a famous illustrator for the British magazine *Punch*. He drew most of the magazine covers.

When Conan was ten the family decided to send him to Hodder preparatory school in Liverpool, England. It was a Catholic school run by Jesuit priests.

Like most boys, Conan at first missed his mother and brothers and sisters. He could go home for only one six-week holiday each year. He was glad that he was tall and large-framed for his age. He was less susceptible to bullies than the smaller boys.

When he was twelve, Conan graduated from Hodder and was sent to Stonyhurst. Stonyhurst was also a Jesuit school and was housed in a medieval castle with marble floors. Conan thought it looked like something out of a Sir Walter Scott novel.

Winter wind cut through the drafty old castle during the punishing winters. Food was minimal, usually dry bread: hot, watered down milk; butter; and potatoes. Conan was always hungry and constantly schemed to have the sweets and extras that only the wealthier boys could buy.

Even with this meager diet, Conan continued to grow. By thirteen, he was five feet, nine inches and fairly stout. Eventually, Conan would grow to be six feet, two inches tall.

Conan blossomed in one critical way during his years at Stonyhurst. To be a good writer means you have to be a good storyteller. It was at Stonyhurst that Conan's gift for telling stories grew. His letters home were full of marvelous scenes and description. Teachers and family encouraged his talent.

Conan began to make plans for his writing. For years he had watched his father give away his paintings whenever someone admired them. Conan was going to be more clever than that. If people enjoyed hearing his stories so much, why shouldn't they be willing to pay for them? He began making money by writing verses that mocked the harsher teachers and selling them to fellow students.

The environment around Stonyhurst began firing Conan's imagination. In Edinburgh he had dreamed about medieval knights in conflict. Stonyhurst had once had actual knights roaming the same grounds he now played cricket on. When he told his mates stories, he brought history to life among the cold, stone walls. He loved it when his audience held their breath, just like he had when The Ma'am had told him a story back home in their kitchen.

Conan loved history. It was something he'd been taught to love by his mother. When he made up stories, they were usually based on events from his history books. He took historical events and changed them to make them his own. Always there was an adventure involved, or a mystery to be solved. His friends relied on Conan's imagination for entertainment. The boys loved Conan's tales, and he loved to make them up for an audience.

But Conan made them pay for their entertainment. That was the only way they could stay and hear his stories. Now he could have the pastries and sweets he craved but had not been able to afford. It was the first money Conan ever earned—and it was so easy for him! "At school," he remembered later, "I could start a hero off from home and carry him through an interminable succession of wayside happenings which would, if necessary, last through the spare hours of a whole term. This faculty remained with me all my school days."

Conan always had trouble following the strict rules laid down the Jesuit masters. His antics often got him in trouble. One of his most frequent crimes was whispering to others during mass. Sometimes he did it deliberately to show the priests he did not fear them. Punishment was swift and certain. A fat square of India rubber, as big as a shoe, slapped his palm. If slapped enough, his hand would be so bruised and swollen he couldn't turn the door handle afterwards. But he refused to cry out during punishment—he was modeling himself on his favorite heroes. "I went out of my way to do really mischievous and outrageous things simply to show that my spirit was unbroken," he said. He wanted them to see—just like he'd shown bullies on the streets of Edinburgh—that he wouldn't be "cowed by violence."

Conan was a mystery to the determined priests. He was smart and capable, but seemingly disobedient. The priests predicted failure for Arthur Conan Doyle. Conan seethed at their rebukes. He also began nursing a disenchantment with Catholicism.

When he was fifteen, Conan visited his Uncle Richard in London. London was then the largest city in the world and it was his first trip to the huge city. He arrived on a frigid

Conan's first trip to London was paid for by his Uncle Richard.

night. The train was unheated and he shivered all the way. But, watching the other passengers intrigued him so that he soon forgot his discomfort.

Conan wound a red muffler around his neck in hopes Uncle Richard would recognize him at the station. He was embarrassed to arrive with his wrists plainly jutting too far below his coat sleeves. Maybe no one would notice. His family could hardly spare money for new clothes.

The next day, Uncle Richard took Conan out to buy him a new winter coat that fit. Conan spent two thrilling weeks being shown around the city that years later would claim him as an honored son. Conan would one day be one of the reasons sightseers would clamor to visit London!

London was so much bigger than Edinburgh. There were wonderful cathedrals, a zoo, palaces, art and history museums, lush hotels, elegant men's stores on Bond Street, fancy tea rooms, galleries and theaters. Conan went to the theater and saw two plays, *Hamlet* and *Our American Cousin* (the play Abraham Lincoln was watching the night he was assassinated at Ford Theater in Washington) with his uncles and aunt.

Conan liked Madame Tussaud's famous wax museum most of all. It was a dark rabbit warren of realistic statues of murderers and victims. He fired off a letter to his mother describing the eerie rooms of horror. Soon, the figures began to appear in his storytelling, as did London's infamous, fog and the shrouded figures making their way along the crowded streets.

By night, walking along gas-lit streets with thickening mists rising off the river Thames, Conan imagined all sorts of scenes.

Back at Stonyhurst, he threw himself into his studies. He took final exams on all his subjects: chemistry, mathematics, foreign languages, English and philosophy. He won top honors. Even his strictest teachers were impressed—and shocked—at how he excelled.

Conan's scores surprised even him. "I was no good at either classics or mathematics; even my English I wrote as pleasure, not as work," he said. But he absorbed everything, made a habit of memorizing favorite poems, and could translate works from several languages.

Conan applied himself most diligently to his favorite pastime, cricket. He loved the rough and tumble of all contact sports.

After earning such high test scores, Conan's uncles wondered if he should study medicine. But he graduated from Stonyhurst at only sixteen. No one would trust a teenage physician. The uncles and The Ma'am decided he should postpone college for a year. Instead, he was sent to study at another Jesuit school in Austria where he could master German, something that would be useful in his medical studies.

Conan's new school was set in another castle. He liked it more than Stonyhurst. The priests were less severe, and the food much better. He studied hard that year and enjoyed himself. He tackled playing the tuba, but music was one thing he had no affinity for. He abandoned the tuba and returned to something he knew more about—writing—and started a student newspaper. He and his friends wrote about anything that caught their interest. Then his stories became too outrageous for the Catholic school, and the priests closed it down. His short career as an editor was over.

After his year in Austria, he returned to Scotland. On the way home to Edinburgh, Conan detoured to Paris to finally meet his Uncle Michael face to face.

His uncle had read all of his godson's letters and verses. He recognized Conan's literary talents. During their visit, he urged Conan to become a writer. But The Ma'am desperately wanted him to be a doctor, and the devoted son would never go against her wishes. He'd won a small scholarship to Edinburgh University that would almost meet his tuition costs, if not his expenses. With luck, he could make it. It looked as if his future was set.

"In 1876," he said later, "I drifted into the study of medicine. The reason largely was that my people lived in Edinboro [sic]—and there is a famous medical school there."

Chapter Three

On the Brink of a Brilliant Idea

Conan was seventeen when he entered medical school in 1876 at Edinburgh University. He studied for four years. During summers he found work assisting physicians. Though it helped him gain some experience, most of the jobs offered no pay, and he was unhappy as an assistant.

When he wasn't studying or working, Conan was writing. In 1879 he sold his first story. The *Chambers Journal* paid three guineas for "The Mystery of Sasassa Valley." "After receiving that little check I was a beast that has once tasted blood . . . I had once proved I could earn gold, and the spirit was in me to do it again . . . I had to earn money by some form of work, and that (writing) was the sort of work I longed to do."

Later that year, he sold another story to a competing magazine. This one, an adventure story, was called "The American's Tale." Although Conan had never been to America, he was fascinated by it and based many of his stories there. The money from the sale of the stories was a godsend. His father's health had now failed completely.

Charles Doyle had been taken to a convalescent home. By age twenty Conan was the oldest male of a family of seven. His sisters Annette and Connie worked as governesses in Europe and sent all their wages home to The Ma'am.

Conan dreamed of the day he could buy his mother fine clothing and provide her with an easier life. He wrote to her devotedly, telling her his dreams for their future. He loved her deeply and admired her large, uncomplaining spirit. The Ma'am savored his letters and kept each one until the end of her life, as if she knew he would become famous. (She amassed about 1,500 letters from her son by the time she died at age ninety.)

Though he was studying to be a doctor, there were other, yet unseen benefits to Conan's medical studies. Science and technical study had refined his mind in important ways and would benefit his writing in a way he would never have suspected. He was learning the technical skills that would one day make him a fortune.

The strongest influence on his future, both as a doctor and as a writer, came from one of the medical school's lecturers. Dr. Joseph Bell was thin, dark, and wiry, with "penetrating gray eyes, angular shoulders, and a jerky way of walking." Bell didn't look or act like other people. He was mysterious and brilliant.

Bell liked Conan and chose him as his assistant. It was an opportunity for the young student to learn how to be a doctor. Conan interviewed patients and briefed Dr. Bell before he examined them.

Conan as a nineteen-year-old student at Edinburgh University.

It was when Conan took his notes in for Dr. Bell to read, or when he sat in during a patient's examination, that he learned the most important lesson from his teacher. Dr. Bell taught Conan how to observe. When he saw a patient, Bell didn't just see the disease or illness. He saw the total person in minute detail. He amazed Conan by pointing out details about a patient that would escape the notice of most people. He was always accurate. In addition to his analysis of medical problems, Bell could usually name the person's profession, habits, and travel destinations after simply observing. This talent for observation made a powerful impression on Conan.

Later, when Conan wrote *A Study in Scarlet*, the first Sherlock Holmes story, he knew who would be the model for his detective. He was tired of the haphazard way that fictional detectives usually solved their crimes. He wanted a much more rigorous, disciplined approach to be used by his hero. He was thrashing about, trying to create a character who could incorporate this method and still be entertaining when: "I thought of my old teacher, Joe Bell, of his eagle face, of his curious ways, and of his eerie trick of spotting details. If he were a detective, he would surely reduce this fascinating but unorganized business to something nearer to an exact science. I would try if I could to get this effect. It was surely possible in real life, so why should I not make it plausible in fiction?" Conan's gratitude for the example of his old teacher was so deep that throughout his writing career, he kept a portrait of Bell in his study.

Other men who went on to be writers also studied at Edinburgh University. J.M. Barrie, who wrote *Peter Pan*, and Robert Louis Stevenson, who wrote many tales such as *Kidnapped* and *Treasure Island*, both trained at the school. Although the three were all close to one another in age, and later said they probably studied at about the same time, they did not meet at Edinburgh. (Doyle never actually met Stevenson, but they wrote several letters to one another, praising each other's work.)

When Barrie and Stevenson first came across the character of Sherlock Holmes in the magazine stories, they both realized instantly that the brilliant hero was modeled after Dr. Bell, whom they had also studied under.

During medical school, Conan had to find ways to make money. He soon found a way to earn some and to have an adventure at the same time. He signed on a whaling ship as the ship's surgeon.

Early in 1880, Doyle set sail for the Arctic. He kept a journal during the voyage. "There are eight boats to a whaler, the eighth, which is kept as a sort of emergency boat, is manned by the so-called 'idlers of the ship. These consisted, in this case, of myself, the steward, the second engineer, and an old seaman. But it happened that, with the exception of the seaman, we were all young and strong and keen; and I think our boat was as good as any."

The Arctic vistas would haunt him all his life. He loved its dry crispness and isolation. His shipmates had plenty of wild stories to tell. They were rough characters, and they teased and taunted Conan, whom they first viewed as a tender, over-educated college student. But he had dealt with roughnecks before, and soon won their acceptance.

This voyage was, he said, "a delightful period of my life." And his earnings aboard ship let Conan put aside some extra money for his family.

After seven months Conan returned to school, where he worked between studies so he could continue on with his plans to be a physician. Finally, after four years of medical school, he graduated in 1881. Conan was now twenty-two. He still did not have enough money to set-up his own practice, and there were few job offers for a recently graduated doctor.

Then Conan had an opportunity to take another post as ship's doctor. He figured that spending a year or two on this voyage might earn him enough money to begin his own practice.

This time Conan sailed Africa's west coast on a much more luxurious passenger ship than on the Arctic voyage. It should have been a more enjoyable trip. But the softness of the experience repelled him. He discovered that his principal duty was to be a companion to the ship's captain. He'd preferred the ruggedness of the whaling ship.

Suddenly the cruise encountered a problem. The seas were rough, and most of the passengers became seasick. Conan came down with tropical fever and nearly died. He could barely help himself, much less his passengers. When a fellow sailor died, Conan wrote that he supposed he could call himself lucky to survive. He sent home dejected verses and dispirited letters.

Conan returned to England in four months. He had not found the same joy in Africa as in the Arctic. His plan to make enough money to begin a practice had also not worked out. He needed to find another way to get his career started.

Chapter Four

The Birth of Sherlock Holmes

Conan decided to join an existing practice, in hopes of some day having his own. Because the town of Southsea could not support his medical career, he moved to Birmingham, England, and worked alongside another doctor among the poor in that dirty, industrial city. However, he soon discovered that he could barely survive on his earnings. It was time to find another place to establish a medical practice.

Then, an old medical school contact, Dr. George Budd, persuaded him to come to the town of Plymouth and work with him in his thriving practice. Conan had helped Budd in the past, and Budd said he wanted to repay his favors. Conan agreed to join him. He thought the situation looked hopeful. He was impressed that Budd had so many poor patients. Surely, most of them could not afford to pay. The idea of working for a doctor who donated his services excited Doyle. This was the kind of medicine he wanted to practice.

Dr. Budd turned out to be a thief and a cheat. It was true that he did not charge a fee for his services, which filled the medical offices with patients. But once the patients were in his examing room, he prescribed unnecessary and expensive medicines that he dispensed himself. This way he was able to gouge big profits from his patients without charging fees. Usually, the unsuspecting paid.

Conan was uncomfortable with Budd's ethics. Budd and his wife also sneaked into Conan's room and read his personal letters. Budd's deceptions became too outrageous for Conan to accept, and he soon left.

Conan's brother Innes came to stay with him, and they moved from Plymouth to Portsmouth, where Conan decided to setup his own medical practice.

It was difficult trying to start a medical practice, however. He could barely afford to furnish a waiting room and a study. With the last of his money, he bought a bed, table, a few chairs, and a little carpet. Then he sat in his rooms, waiting for patients to come along but few did.

Conan hated the boredom of waiting. He had too much time on his hands so he began filling his days by writing. He worked out his stories in longhand as he waited for the patients who seldom arrived. Soon the writing was more profitable than medicine. When his money was gone, he managed to get an advance from a publisher for a story, "My Friend, The Murderer." The advance was not large and the story would earn no more money. He still had no patients and no regular income.

Many days Conan and Innes could not afford food, and never fresh vegetables. They lived on tea, bacon, and an occasional fish. To make ends meet Conan and Innes took in a couple of boarders, but they did not stay long. Nothing seemed to work. The few patients who came in the door were indigent and couldn't pay.

Conan was unsure of his future as a doctor; the only thing he excelled at other than medicine was writing. Maybe he could sell more stories? Write a novel? He could write short stories quickly and get immediate money, but it was difficult to build a reputation with short stories. He could write them forever and never get anywhere, he complained to The Ma'am.

Conan spent some of his free time playing cricket, rugby and soccer. He didn't like to sit back and watch life. He was a participator. He also went to meetings of the Portsmouth Literary and Scientific Society.

Then, one day, he got a patient. Jack Hawkins had advanced epilepsy. It was soon evident that he was terminal. After spending several weeks as a resident patient in Conan's house, Hawkins died. Louise Hawkins, Jack's sister, watched Conan take care of her doomed brother and thought he was a kind and compassionate man. Conan began to notice her as well and kept in touch with the family after Jack's death.

Soon Conan was in love with Louise, who was nicknamed "Touie," and he asked The Ma'am to come meet her. When she approved of his choice, he asked Touie's

Conan hard at work in 1888.

mother for her hand in marriage.

The couple married in 1885. Although his practice was still only scraping by, Louise was a comfort during this difficult financial time.

Conan began to sell more short stories. If only they earned more! Touie received a small stipend from a family trust, and it relieved finances a bit for their household. Conan even occasionally treated patients.

It was during these years that Conan was first introduced to a subject that would dominate the last years of this life. Sometime between 1885 and 1887, a patient named General Drayson asked Conan if he was interested in the paranormal. When Conan said he had been intrigued by the possibility of contacting the dead, Drayson took him to some paranormal lectures and to several seances. During this time, seances were popular. People would have friends over for dinner and hold one as part of the evening's entertainment.

General Drayson was an astronomer and mathematician—a man of science, like Conan. Drayson claimed he could communicate with his dead brother, and Conan could not dismiss the idea. After all, what could be more important than discovering proof of life after death? Conan began his own investigations, scientifically observing and recording facts.

Conan listed seventy-four publications on psychic phenomenon in his notebooks and began his research. For six months, he went to seances and wrote about what he saw.

Conan attended his first seance here at General Drayson's house.

He eventually decided he couldn't come to any conclusions. There were no absolutes; it was important to keep an open mind. Although Conan had abandoned his research, this interest in what lay on "the other side" did not leave. It was merely dormant.

Conan decided to write a mystery story with a detective as the central character. He'd always loved Monsieur Dupin, Edgar Allan Poe's detective hero in "The Purloined Letter" and other stories. The detective novels of Charles Dickens' friend Wilkie Collins—*The Moonstone* and *The Woman in White*—had honored places on his bookshelf.

But one thing about many of these detective stories bothered Conan. Why did the detectives always stumble onto their results by luck or by chance? Obviously, real-life detectives weren't always so fortunate. At that very moment, Jack the Ripper eluded Scotland Yard, despite the biggest manhunt in history. It seemed to be a perfect time to show the reading public how a detective may try to think logically when solving a crime. To portray an active detective using his intelligence and powers of observation to solve crimes might be what the public wanted—especially if the detective was highly intelligent. Wouldn't the public's morale be lifted if there was someone, even a fictional character, who could counteract violence?

Why not have a detective that worked in a methodical way, using all the tools and skills available to a modern man? He thought of his old teacher Dr. Bell. He would have made detective work an exact science. There were other qualities about Dr. Bell that could make him an interesting model for a fictional detective. He had been a complicated man—odd-looking, intense, quirky, and strange.

Conan remembered one particular incident. Bell examined a civilian patient with several of his students present. The doctor and patient exchanged quiet words for a few moments. Then Bell turned to the group and announced that the man recently had been discharged from the army. He then told them the regiment his patient was from and that he was a non-commissioned officer. He added, to his students' astonishment, that the man had recently left the island of Barbados in the British West Indies.

The patient confirmed everything that Dr.Bell said. How had Bell known? It was all elementary, he explained. "You see, gentlemen, the man was a very respectful man but did not remove his hat. They do not in the army, but he would have learned civilian ways had he been long discharged. He has an air of authority and is obviously Scottish. As to Barbados, his complaint is elephantiasis, which is West Indian and not British."

To ordinary men, Conan thought, it was all miraculous until Bell had explained his method. Then it seemed simple, even elementary. Conan's character wouldn't just seem clever, he'd give readers real examples of how he did things. He'd show them he was clever.

There were other people Conan thought of while creating his detective. Sir William Arbuthnot Lane was chief of surgery at Guy's Hospital in London. Lane, like Bell, was eccentric, with strong powers of observation.

A fictional character was forming in Doyle's brain. His detective would be a man of science, with a brilliant, penetrating mind. He'd have eyes and ears that missed nothing. He'd be a man to be reckoned with . . . a real detective.

The idea for the style of the stories was borrowed from a French writer, Emile Gaboriau, who neatly dovetailed his plots. (Gaboriau had begun detective fiction a few decades earlier.) Conan worked on, borrowing a little here, a little there, throwing in a dash of the real-life doctors Bell and Lane, whom he'd observe in true life. He worked like Dr. Frankenstein, creating his famous monster from his experiences and books he'd read. At the end, the detective seemed to get up and walk off the page.

When Doyle finished creating the central figure of his mystery story, his detective was big, just like Conan—over six feet tall. His face was razor sharp and thin. He had a hawk's beak of a nose and little intense eyes, hawk-sharp, too. He was unemotional and driven when he worked, but subject to fits of depression when idle. He used cocaine when bored, and sometimes fired his pistol at his apartment walls and ceilings. Conan decided he was the most notorious character ever. His creation scorned women. He'd fear nothing; a driven, conceited, condescending genius— a tortured spirit. His detective was full of shadow and darkness and untidiness. He'd call him . . . Sherringford Holmes. Well, maybe not. Sherringford was a little too

Study in Scarlet

Ormond Sacker - ~~from Sudan~~ from Afghanistan
Lived at 221 B Upper Baker Street
with

J Sherrinford Holmes -

The Laws of Evidence.

Reserved -
Sleepy eyed young man - philosopher - Collector of rare Violins
An Amati - Chemical laboratory

I have four hundred a year -

I am a Consulting detective -

What rot this is " I cried - throwing the volume
: petulantly aside " I must say that I have no
patience with people who build up fine theories in their
own armchairs which can never be reduced to
practice -

Lecoq was a bungler -
Dupin was better. Dupin was decidedly smart -
His trick of following a train of thought was more
sensational than clever but still he had analytical genius

A manuscript page from an early start on *A Study in Scarlet*.

formal a name. What about Sherlock? Conan scribbled some other names on a sheet of notepaper as he thought it over. Finally, he decided on Sherlock. Sherlock was the name for a man of action, of bravado, of mystery.

Conan worked diligently at his writing desk. He would need a narrator at Sherlock Holmes' side. Someone close to Sherlock who could tell of his exploits and triumphs. A sort of comrade and friend, but an ordinary man and foil for this genius Sherlock. The companion needed a plain, honest name. Watson, he thought, would do fine. Dr. John H. Watson, the name and persona of a proper Englishman. It was borrowed from a real John Watson, an old acquaintance.

Now, finally, Conan had, as he said, his "puppets" in Holmes and Watson. He used them in a long story, or novella, called *A Study in Scarlet*. Conan was satisfied with the characters Sherlock Holmes and John Watson. Both were doctors, although Holmes was a scientist and Watson a physician, just like him. Both were clever in their own ways. Where one was the innovator—experimental, daring, bold, self-absorbed and moody—the other was careful, cautious, solidly stable, predictable, and retiring. Together, they were the perfect team. Two halves of a whole.

When the long story was finished, Conan knew the mystery he had written was as good as he could make it. *A Study in Scarlet* was rooted in Mormonism and the American west, still exotic subjects for an English writer.

He sent the first Sherlock Holmes story out, "circling"

An illustration of the first meeting of Holmes and Watson from the American publication of *A Study in Scarlet*.

Conan's list of usual publishers. The first one sent it back after a month. It was too short, he said. Then another rejected it—it was too long. Conan fought off his depression as he collected the rejection letters.

Finally a publisher of what Conan considered to be lesser quality stories accepted it for publication the next year. He was a little embarrassed by the magazine's reputation, and discouraged by the pittance they offered in payment, but if he stuck the story in his desk drawer, no one would ever read it. He was confident that as soon as the public read about Sherlock Holmes, they'd be fascinated by him and want more stories about the strange genius detective.

Chapter Five

Worldwide Celebrity

A Study in Scarlet, was published in 1887 in *Beeton's Christmas Annual*. Conan sold his story for twenty-five pounds. The plot concerned the murder of an American in England. The solution revealed that the motive for the murder was also rooted in America. Conan had been fascinated by the United States since boyhood. The story met with a lukewarm response in his native country, although several critics compared it to Edgar Allan Poe. *A Study in Scarlet* was a bigger success in America, where the publisher asked for another long story.

The next Holmes novella, *The Sign of the Four*, a moody, macabre tale about a stolen treasure and murderous thieves with wooden legs, was published in America and England in 1890. Although it was well-received, and is today considered one of the very best Holmes stories, its publication also earned little notice at the time.

Although devising the plots was sometimes maddening work, Conan wrote the detective stories quickly. This way he had time to work on other fiction. He was convinced that one project, the novel *Micah Clarke*, would be a huge success. The story concerned the adventures of the title character during the seventeenth century conflicts between the Stuarts and the Puritans. This tumultuous period of English history was one of Doyle's favorites. The novel was eventually published to strong reviews and sales.

Once Conan decided to make his living with his pen, he never looked back. After the idea for a story or novel became fixed in his mind, he would sit down and write out the story long-hand. He wrote in a fast moving, first-person narrative style that caused his stories to flow. "I write when the mood is on me," he told an interviewer. "I never dictate a single word, but write the entire story with my pen. I write slowly and very seldom make any corrections afterward. When I have done so, I have found the result so unsatisfactory that I have restored what I had originally written . . . First impressions always seem to me to be best."

His American publisher struck a deal with Conan to write novellas for *Lippincott's Magazine*, a prestigious assignment. Lippincott published other famous British writers, such as Oscar Wilde, who first published his classic novel, *The Picture of Dorian Gray*, in the magazine.

Conan continued to write the Holmes stories, even while working on *Micah Clarke*. The next Sherlock Holmes story published after "The Sign of the Four" burst the eccentric detective into the public imagination. "A Scandal in Bohemia" was first published in a new, soon to be wildly popular British magazine, *The Strand*. The tale involves the

Conan loved all sports throughout his life. He took up bicycling in the 1890s.

efforts of the king of Bohemia to reclaim some compromising photos. The king is to be married soon and wants to regain the images before his wedding. He fears blackmail. The king hires Holmes to find the pictures. The twist of this story is that in the end Holmes is outsmarted by Irene Adler, the king's nemesis, who charms the detective like no other female he encounters. Adler's memory will linger over the rest of his life. The story's opening line is, "To Sherlock Holmes she is always the woman."

When *The Strand* published "A Scandal in Bohemia," some thought they recognized the character of Wilhelm Gottsreich Sigismond von Ormstein, the king of Bohemia, as being a thinly disguised portrait of the current Prince of Wales, the future Edward VII, and the eldest son of Queen Victoria. "Bertie," as the prince was nicknamed, was a notorious gambler, drinker, and womanizer. His affairs with actresses and other women were a constant source of gossip and speculation. Many readers shook their heads knowingly as they read about a member of a royal family desperately trying to stop a scandal from erupting from his indiscretions.

Although there is no evidence that Conan planned for the story to reflect the current gossip, he certainly benefited from it. The issue of *The Strand* containing "A Scandal in Bohemia" literally flew off the news stands, and the editor begged Conan for more Sherlock Holmes stories. Five more swiftly followed: "The Red-headed League," "A Case of Identity," "The Five Orange Pips," "The Man with

The cover page for the *Beeton's Christmas Annual* of 1887.

the Twisted Lip," and "The Boscombe Valley Mystery."

Suddenly, Conan was financially comfortable—and more requests for Holmes stories came. Seizing on his new popularity, Conan demanded fifty pounds for future stories, triple what the earlier ones earned. The editor agreed and contracted with him to write six more adventures.

There was one problem with Conan's success with the Sherlock Holmes stores. He was quickly growing weary of his detective and began speaking of him disparagingly as "a calculating machine." He wanted to devote more time to his first love, historical novels. But the financial rewards were too good to refuse. Besides, he could turn out a Holmes story in a week. In the fall of 1891, he completed "The Adventure of the Blue Carbuncle" and "The Adventure of the Speckled Band" in seven days. Both are two of Conan's best stories, portraying Holmes at his most brilliant.

Conan hurried to finish the stories in 1891 so he could re-dedicate himself to a historical novel, *The White Company*, that he always considered to be his best work. *The White Company* reflected his love for the novels of Sir Walter Scott. Just as in *Ivanhoe*, it is a story of knights and chilvalry. Unlike the earlier novel, however, *The White Company* is much more historically accurate, as it traces the exploits of a company of knights as they joust and fight for glory in France during the Hundred Years War of the fourteenth century.

Conan worked long hours every day. He moved smoothly between the novels he loved and the detective stories he

The future Edward VII when he was still the Prince of Wales. Conan may have based the character of Wilhelm Gottsreich Sigismond von Ormstein on the playboy prince.

wrote for money. But even with his phenomenal ability, Conan could not write the stories fast enough. To ensure a steady supply of the necessary plots, he began clipping news stories about strange and unsolved crimes. He carefully catalogued and arranged these real mysteries. When creating a plot he began by solving the problem first. Then he back-tracked through the evolution of the solution to create the most baffling way to introduce the mystery to the reader.

After finishing the six contracted stories, Conan had more important things to do with his talents than wasting them on Sherlock Holmes. He decided to demand so much money that *The Strand* would have to stop badgering him for more detective stories. He raised his asking price to about 5,000 pounds for twelve more Holmes stories. He also insisted that he would determine their length. The editor stunned him by saying that would be perfectly fine. After regaining his composure, Conan wrote some of the very best Sherlock Holmes tales, including "The Gloria Scott," "The Crooked Man," "The Musgrave Ritual," and nine others.

Conan may have felt overshadowed by Sherlock Holmes and written the stories solely for the money, but the neurotic detective made him a celebrity. He was invited to become a member of the Idler's, a group of famous British writers that included J.M. Barrie, Rudyard Kipling, and George Bernard Shaw among its members. His income shot up to around 16,000 British pounds (at the time over $15,000,

Rudyard Kipling was Conan's life-long friend.

an extraordinary salary for 1890.) He hobnobbed with the rich and famous—all thanks to his despised detective.

Soon after the stories began appearing, letters addressed to Sherlock Holmes filled Conan's mailbox. The letters concerned all kinds of dilemmas, or what Conan called "singular cases." Pleas for help with disappearances, murders, and stolen treasures were commonplace. Conan answered as many as possible, always emphasizing there was no real Sherlock Holmes. Then, teasingly, he signed his responses "Dr. John Watson."

Scotland Yard consulted with Conan, seeking his help in solving the unsolvable cases. Although Sherlock Holmes spoke contemptuously of Scotland Yard, the stories enhanced the police agency's reputation. Conan made sure to call Scotland Yard "the finest police in the world" in his own pronouncements.

Conan was delighted to consult with William Burns, who ran a detective agency in the United States. He learned a great deal about crime solving from spending time with real detectives. In the course of writing his stories, he had shown professionals a new scientific, methodical way to approach detective work that was changing the way they performed their jobs, and they always showed him great respect in return.

Chapter Six

Reichenbach Falls

In the winter of 1893, Conan and Louise traveled to Switzerland. Their second child, Kingsley, had been born the year before, and Louise had not yet regained her strength. She was often wracked with a cough. They hoped the dry, cold mountain air would be good for her.

They battled snowstorms on the trip, and the freezing weather seemed to have a worsening effect on Louise's cough. It was difficult to enjoy the beauty of the snow-covered Alps. One highlight of the trip was a visit to Oberland, where the couple stared in fascination at the 300-foot Reichenbach Falls. The swirling, turbulent waters matched their mood as they fretted over Louise's health.

Louise's health continued to worsen. They decided to cut short their trip and return to London to seek special medical care. There the doctor discovered blood in her sputum and, after further tests, diagnosed Louise as suffering from tuberculosis. There was no vaccine for the disease in the nineteenth century. She was terminally ill.

Conan's reaction to the news was to plunge into work.

Over the next weeks his children, Mary Louise and Kingsley, later recalled he spent most of his waking hours working away behind his locked study door. The children were cared for by his mother-in-law, Mrs. Hawkins. Occasionally, he and Touie took long trips to Switzerland and Egypt to seek a healthful climate.

On one trip to Switzerland, Conan decided to try his imported Norwegian skis. Skis had not yet been used for sport in the Alps. He teamed up with a couple of villagers and skied cross-country from the Swiss villages of Davos to Arosa. Conan ended the last treacherous descent of the twelve-mile journey on the seat of his Harris tweed pants. He joked afterwards that Harris tweeds weren't as invincible as they were advertised to be. But a new sport—skiing— had been introduced to the Swiss.

The trips with Touie and the skiing, however, were only brief diversions for Conan. He could not escape the guilt he felt over his wife's illness. Busy writing the Holmes stories, he—a doctor, no less!—had ignored the signs of Louise's illness. How could he have been so blind? All because he was working on those blasted detective stories.

He tired of writing about Holmes. By this time, collections of the stories were being published the world over. Sherlock Holmes stories had been translated into many languages, and his audience was now so vast it knew no bounds. There would always be money in Holmes and Watson, even if he never wrote another story.

Conan decided to end the series in a way that left no doubt

as to his intention. He would be finished with Mr. Sherlock Holmes of 221B Baker Street and his friend Dr. John Watson, forever. He knew killing Holmes would generate controversy. "It was still the Sherlock Holmes stories for which the public clamoured," he said ruefully, although he considered them to be the lesser of his works. "I do not wish to be ungrateful to Holmes," he continued. "If I have sometimes been inclined to weary of him, it is because his character admits of no light or shade."

How does one do away with an almost superhumanly intelligent sleuth? Conan couldn't have Holmes shot or stabbed. Holmes deserved a better death than that. Then he remembered the sad trip he and Louise had taken to Switzerland, and the fearsome Reichenbach Falls. The falls were "a worthy tomb for poor Sherlock, even if I buried my banking account along with him," he decided.

In "The Final Problem," published in the *Strand* magazine in 1893, Sherlock Holmes encounters the evil genius Professor James Moriarity, a man as doggedly evil as Holmes is good. Holmes, with Watson in tow, track this "Napoleon of crime" to Switzerland, where they meet and have a final, climactic fight on the dramatic cliffs of Reichenbach Falls. This action scene takes place "off stage" because Watson, the narrator, is tricked into returning to the hotel so Moriarity can more easily attack Holmes.

Watson returns from his useless trip to discover Sherlock's silver cigarette case and a note Holmes left before falling to his death over the pounding, misty falls.

The death of Sherlock Holmes shocked Conan's readers. The whole nation grieved. Young men went to work in London's financial district with black mourning bands around their arms. Conan received letters beginning with "You Brute!" He later remarked that he suddenly realized that a man was never really appreciated until his death. "I heard of many who wept," he marveled, at the news of Sherlock's death.

But Conan was not among them. Personally, he said, he was glad to move into "new fields of imagination." There was only one regret from this man who had spent so many years living in poverty. "High prices [for the stories] made it difficult to get one's thoughts away from Holmes," he admitted.

After the death of Holmes, Conan immediately turned his attention to the stage. Since he had been a teenager, Conan had a passion for the theater. In 1894 he wrote a short play, *Waterloo*. It was produced and acted by Sir Henry Irving, the reigning genius of English theater. It was first performed at the Prince's Theatre in Bristol, England, and was well received. Maybe there was life for Conan Doyle and his writing career after the tragic death of Sherlock Holmes.

Chapter Seven

New Love

Sherlock Holmes made Conan a public figure. He toured Britain and gave readings and discussed his writings. He enjoyed meeting his readers and the trips were profitable. At first he found standing on a stage before hundreds of assembled people difficult, but he overcame his dread. He set about public speaking with the same determination he devoted to other challenges and learned to compensate for his shyness. He grew into an entertaining speaker and was soon in high demand.

An American promoter, Major Pond, clamored for Doyle to come to the United States. He assured Conan there was a huge audience of people anxious to meet him. Conan was proud to be asked and always wanted to widen the audience for his work. It seemed like too good an offer to refuse.

Conan would have to leave Louise behind. She was too frail to travel. She encouraged him to go. Relatives could stay with her, and she did not want to deny him this opportunity. Conan asked his brother Innes to join him on his first trip to America.

Conan and Innes Doyle sailed for the United States in the autumn of 1894. The journey was exciting and exhausting. Conan gave over forty readings from his lecture series "Facts about Fiction" throughout the Midwest.

Conan was impressed by American ingenuity. He wrote to a friend at home, "We've got to go into partnership with them or be overshadowed by them." The American public in turn was wowed by the tall, composed, distinguished-looking author.

Conan loved that he could take a morning train from New York City and follow the scenic and beautiful Hudson River northward. Before evening he could be in upstate New York, where the Huron Indians and the Canadians had battled. Then, he said, he could be in the Adirondack forests by evening, where bear and panther lurked. It felt, he said, like gliding on a back eddy left by the stream of civilization. As he had as a boy in the cold Stonyhurst castle, Conan soon romanticized his surroundings, imagining fierce warriors and fur-clad trappers in the vivid woods.

At the end of an evening's talk, Conan wanted to slip away through the stage doors to avoid the waiting throngs. But his promoter had assured fans there would be question-and-answer sessions afterwards. Conan didn't want to face the audiences individually. "I haven't the courage to look anybody in the face," he said to Pond.

The most delightful part of the trip was an encounter with a cabman. What transpired during this meeting became a fixed part of Conan's lecture for years afterward. Doyle arrived at the Boston train station before a speech to the Aldine Club and hailed a cabman with a "dog-earred" book in his breast pocket. He asked the cabbie to take him to either of two addresses—he wasn't sure if Major Pond would be at his hotel or at his club waiting.

The cabbie asked his pardon once they were in the car and said, "I think you'll find Major Pond awaiting you at Parker's, Sir." Conan stared, speechless, at the driver. They drove to Parker's and, sure enough, Pond was there. The cabman helped Conan from the car, and then refused to accept his fare. He politely asked for tickets to Conan's lecture instead.

Conan had no idea the cabman had recognized him and insisted the man tell him how he knew his passenger was Conan Doyle. "Come, come, I am not accustomed to being beaten at my own tricks," Conan said. "Tell me how you ascertained who I am, and you shall have tickets for your whole family and such cigars as you smoke here in America, besides."

The cabbie beamed and said: "If you will excuse the personal remarks, your coat lapels are badly downward, where they have been grasped by the pertinacious New York reporters. Your hair has the Quakerish cut of the Philadelphia barber, and your hat, battered at the brim in front, shows where you have tightly grasped it, in the struggle to stand your ground at a Chicago literary luncheon. Your right overshoe has a large block of Buffalo mud just under the instep, the odor of a Utica cigar hangs about your clothing, and the overcoat itself shows the slovenly brushing of the porters of the through sleepers from Albany. The crumbs of doughnut on the top of your bag—pardon me, your luggage—could only have come there in Springfield, and stencilled upon the very end of the Wellington, in fairly plain lettering, is the name, Arthur Conan Doyle."

The Boston cabbie had out-Sherlocked Conan Doyle! Then the cabman beamed and made another confession. He was a member of the Cabmen's Literary Guild and knew the writer would be arriving that day. Doyle roared with laughter at the man's wit.

The trip was great fun, but Conan received a blow shortly before he was to sail for home. His friend, Robert Louis Stevenson, who had suffered poor health most of his life, died in his adopted home of Samoa. The two had been writing each other (they never met face-to-face) in mutual admiration for each other's writings. Stevenson joked that when Doyle waved the "white plume" of his pen, he felt compelled to write and compete with him. The result was Stevenson's famous book, *Treasure Island.*

When Stevenson died, his family asked Conan if he could complete an unfinished work, the novel *St. Ives.* A heartbroken Conan felt he couldn't do it and asked that they find another writer to manage it. "Something seemed to have passed out of my world when Stevenson died," Conan said.

Once back in England, Conan turned his attention to

Robert Louis Stevenson died at his home in Samoa.

Touie. They continued to take trips to other countries, such as Egypt, seeking a healthier climate for her illness. But Conan eventually became convinced by an expert on tuberculosis that the climate in Surrey County southwest of London would be just as healing as any in the world.

His architect friend, William Ball, designed and built a home for them in Surrey County. Conan and Touie named the house "Undershaw" and moved in the fall of 1896.

Despite Touie's poor health, Conan tried to fill his life with work and amusements. He loved model trains and constructed a miniature monorail on the grounds for his children. He got the idea from his new friend, the young writer H.G. Wells.

In 1897, Queen Victoria celebrated her diamond jubilee, marking fifty years the tiny monarch had ruled Great Britain. The entire empire celebrated; all of England was excited. It was during this time of festivities, when Conan was thirty-eight, that he met someone who would bring him more joy and—at least for the next ten years—more frustration than anyone else in his life.

Jean Leckie, a friend of Conan's sister, Lottie, was the daughter of a wealthy Scotsman. She lived nearby in Glebe and enjoyed an active outdoor life, full of hunting, riding, and other sports. Blonde, with green eyes and a pale complexion, Jean had trained her fine singing voice at schools in Germany and Italy. She was fourteen years younger than Conan.

Conan fell in love with her immediately. Soon it was

Conan fell in love with Jean Leckie in the summer of 1897.

evident that she returned his feelings.

Conan's passion for Jean Leckie tested his commitment to the knightly, chivalrous ideal that he held so dear. There had been a tradition in the middle ages of love stories and songs dealing with "impossible love." Usually social barriers, such as marriage, kept the lovers apart. Conan, who romanticized the medieval period, now had a chance to play out a version of this old morality tale.

Conan was obligated to Touie. He was bound by his principles to not disgrace her in any way. To divorce her for another woman was impossible. He also would do nothing to bring dishonor on Jean. He explained his position to Jean, and told her that he thought she should find someone else. She refused. She would wait for Conan to be free. So began ten years of frustration for them both.

In 1899, a famous American actor, William Gillette, wrote Conan to ask for permission to bring Sherlock Holmes to the stage in America. Since his play, *Waterloo*, had been a success, Conan was intrigued. But Gillette wanted to change the character of Holmes a bit—maybe even create a romantic interest for the bachelor detective. Conan did not reject the idea outright, and Gillette traveled to England and met Conan. They instantly liked one another. Conan agreed to dramatize Sherlock Holmes and agreed to most of Gillette's requests—except one. There would be no romantic interest for Holmes. Doyle knew that a great deal of the detective's appeal was his eccentricity. Matching him with a love interest would make him too normal.

William Gillette convinced Conan to allow him to bring Sherlock Holmes to the United States in 1899.

Conan's collaboration with William Gillette was presented on stage in 1899. By then it had been six long years since his fans had a taste of their favorite detective. The play, called simply *Sherlock Holmes*, was a huge success. Would it be possible, Conan's anxious editors asked, that this success would convince him that he must write more stories about the resident of 221 B Baker Street?

Chapter Eight

Sir Arthur

In the same year Sherlock Holmes returned to the stage, Britain suddenly found itself fighting a war thousands of miles away on a distant continent. A century earlier, Britain had seized part of Southern Africa from the Dutch in order to protect its sea routes. The Dutch Boer settlers—"Boer" is a Dutch word meaning "farmer"—who lived in the seized area resented British control and fled to the interior. There they settled two new areas they called the Orange Free State and the South African Republic. However, Britain, afraid of the growing strength of the Dutch settlers and eager to control the vast natural resources, eventually seized part of this new territory too. The Dutch fought back and regained their independence. But by the turn of the century, as English imperialists like Cecil Rhodes advocated expansion of the British empire in Africa, the Boers again felt their land was being threatened and declared war against the British.

As news of the Boers' actions reached England, patriotism swept through the country. At the time, the island nation was the most powerful on earth. London was the largest city, and the center of commerce and culture for much of the western world. Dealing with the upstart Boers promised to be a rollicking good time.

Conan was caught up in the enthusiasm. In a letter to a local newspaper, Conan wrote that Britain's sportsmen—those who could ride and shoot—should join in the fight against the Boers. And Conan felt he should join them. He wrote a letter to his mother: "I have perhaps the strongest influence over young men, especially young sporting men, of anyone in England bar Kipling. That being so, it is really important that I should give them a lead."

Conan tried to sign up as a volunteer. But because of his age—he was forty—he was rejected. Instead, he was offered a chance to help manage a field hospital in the South African town of Bloemfontein. He and a friend would be in charge of the fifty-bed hospital.

An excited Conan sailed for South Africa on February 28, 1900. The trip over was uneventful, and he disembarked impatient to get on with the work of saving soldiers lives. But his excitement soon waned. It was his first experience with the realities of war. The hospital, a series of tents set up in an open field, was overrun with soldiers, many of them suffering not from wounds but from a vile contagious fever. There was precious little disinfectant or clean linens for the beds. Rain was constant, and thick mud was everywhere. The flies were unstoppable.

Conan kept a diary and in one passage wrote that "one man died as I fanned him. I saw the light go out of his eyes."

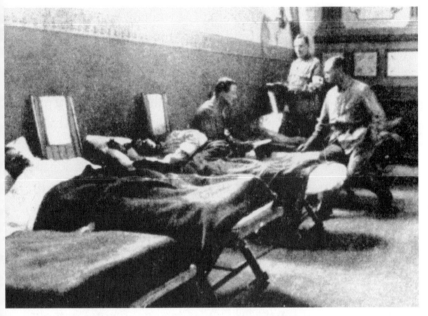

Conan (sitting on bed) during his service at Bloemfontein.

Conditions, overall, were utterly miserable.

Conan stayed and worked all day and night, using his rusty medical skills, for seven months. When he returned home, he wrote about his experiences in numerous articles that described how antiquated tactics had caused great loss of life to the Boers. Most of these were published in *The Strand* magazine.

In one article, he even chastised the military training that British soldiers received. Conan thought that all men ought to have firearms training to prepare them for battle. He had observed British soldiers in showy uniforms armed with sabers and swords being cut down by Boers with rifles. It was an outrage to him. He personally organized rifle clubs throughout Britain, the first at Undershaw. Conan paid for the costs of the rifles and targets himself.

Conan was consumed with tactical issues regarding the military. But the central question of the so-called Boer War for many was more a question of ethics than strategy. In South Africa, wartime atrocities had been committed by the British. They ruthlessly pursued victory by burning farms and homes, destroying crops and causing widespread starvation. Slowly, this "scorched earth" policy broke the backs of the agrarian Boers. Captured Boers numbering in the hundreds of thousands were herded into British concentration camps where they suffered, starved, and many died. British militia were charged with raping Boer women and even bayoneting their children.

As news of this swept across Europe, many grew outraged and demanded an end to the war. Anti-war protesters held meetings in Germany, where protestors were particularly vocal.

Conan defended Great Britain's war performance in a pamphlet called "The Great Boer War." Another writer, William Stead, had written his own booklet, sharply critical of what he considered British aggression. Stead was supported by many prominent writers and intellectuals, such as George Bernard Shaw.

Conan grew more and more strident in his support for the British war effort. Soon he became a "lightning rod" for those who thought Britain was behaving brutally. The public debate raged. Now Doyle was internationally famous, and his opinion on subjects mattered to a great number of people. He made some important friends who encouraged him to get involved in politics. They felt that his strong, pro-military voice was needed in the Parliament.

Conan hesitated to enter politics. He knew that he was now a highly controversial figure. He could be subjected to some ugly attacks as tensions over the war increased. Also, running for office would take him away from his work and his family. He knew that his time with Louise was limited. But, in the end, the opportunity to be heard on the important issues of his day was too large a temptation to ignore. He decided to throw his hat into the ring.

In late 1900 Doyle ran for a seat in the House of Commons, the lower house of the British Parliament. He ran as a Liberal Unionist, someone opposed to allowing Ireland to break away from Great Britain and form its own nation. He also continued speaking up for the war effort. He ran to represent Edinburgh, his hometown. He knew going in that his chances were limited. Edinburgh was radical, and Conan was moderately conservative. He ran a spirited campaign, however, and never flinched from delivering his message, even in areas where he knew it was highly unpopular. Conan lost in a close election.

Even after his political defeat, Conan continued to influence public opinion. He still wielded the power of the pen. He spoke out on tax and social reform. Most surprisingly, he worked in the controversial movement to change divorce laws. Why should people remain trapped by antiquated laws in unhappy marriages? Other countries had relaxed their divorce laws without moral ruin. Conan believed Britain should stop making divorce difficult and sometimes impossible. Many prominent people, such as the archbishop of Canterbury, the spiritual leader of the Church of England, disagreed. But Conan stood firm. Eventually, divorce laws were liberalized.

After the huge success in the United States of *Sherlock Holmes*, the stage play came to London and again was a huge success. Doyle began to feel the urge to pick up his pen and create another Sherlock Holmes work. But he hesitated to bring the detective back to life. Maybe it would be possible to set a story in the days before his untimely death in Switzerland.

Conan had been on vacation in the southwest English countryside when he heard a folk legend about a ghostly hound in the nearby moors. The atmosphere was perfect for a moody, creepy story. The temptation to weave a yarn around such a setting was impossible to resist. He set immediately to work. At first he had no intention of using Holmes in the story. But as it became evident that he was writing a mystery he saw no reason to reinvent a detective when he already had the best-known puzzle solver in the world. The result was a Holmes novel called *The Hound of the Baskervilles* that was serialized in *The Strand* in 1901.

Needless to say, it was a great success. Sherlock Holmes was back and more popular than ever. People lined up at newsstands to buy the magazine. *The Hound of the*

Baskervilles was to become perhaps the most famous of all the Sherlock Holmes stories. The success of this was so overwhelming that even Doyle eventually gave in to public clamor. More Holmes stories appeared in *The Strand* for the next few years.

In 1902, Conan disputed author William Stead in another work called *The War in South Africa: Its Cause and Conduct*, a 60,000-word defense of his country's political and military actions in the Boer War. He also resorted to something that he used many times during his life in aid of his causes. He printed a public appeal in newspapers asking for donations to raise money to print and distribute *The War in South Africa*. More money than needed was raised.

One contributor was the new king, Edward VII, the former Prince or Wales who many thought was the model for the king of Bohemia in "A Scandal in Bohemia." Conan's work on behalf of the war effort won him an invitation to the new king's coronation.

Prior to the coronation, Edward invited Conan to a palace dinner and had him seated beside him. The king praised his efforts to win support of the war. He was so impressed with Conan's defense of the conflict in South Africa that an offer of knighthood soon followed the dinner.

This was a high honor. But Doyle wrote The Ma'am that he wanted to decline the title. He claimed to not think much of the knighthood. "Surely you don't mean that I should take a knighthood: the badge of the provincial mayor?" he asked. "It is a silently understood thing in this world that the big men . . . do not condescend to such things. Not that I am a big man, but something inside me revolts at the thought. Fancy Rhodes or Chamberlain or Kipling doing such a thing! And why should my standards be lower than theirs? . . . The title I value most is that of Doctor. . ."

The Ma'am argued that to refuse the title would be a direct insult to the king. She won the argument, and on August 9, 1902, Doyle was somewhat reluctantly knighted. "I remember that on going down to Buckingham Palace to receive the accolade, I found that all who were waiting for various honours were herded into funny little pens, according to their style and degree, there to await their turns . . ." he wrote later.

The inscription said Conan was honored for "outstanding service to the nation." King Edward also made him the deputy lieutenant of Surrey. The boy who had dreamed of knights on proud steeds was now Sir Arthur Conan Doyle.

Chapter Nine

Crime Fighter

Doyle continued to hope Touie would regain her health. His training as a doctor, however, did not allow him to ignore the truth. As the tuberculosis progressed, he struggled to be optimistic.

During the last ten years of Touie's life, Doyle's mother knew of his love for Jean Leckie. The Ma'am had met Jean and supported their relationship. She knew that her son believed in strict standards of personal and sexual behavior. She also lived her life with this same code of moral behavior as her guide. As long as Touie lived, The Ma'am knew that Conan would honor his marriage vows. Over the years she grew very fond of Jean, and even occasionally visited her.

As his wife's disease worsened, Doyle wrote The Ma'am that he had "nothing but affection and respect for Touie. I have never in my whole married life had one cross word with her, nor will I ever cause her any pain."

By the summer of 1906, Touie's long struggle was ending. In one of many letters to his brother Innes, Conan wrote: "It may be days, or it may be weeks, but the end now seems inevitable."

During her last days, Touie called her children to her bedside and told them she hoped her father would remarry. Her death came one morning in early July. During the pre-dawn hours, Touie died in her bed with Conan holding her hand. She was forty-nine years old.

After Touie was buried on the grounds of their estate, Conan grieved for many months. Although he had loved Jean for years, his feelings for Touie were deep, and based on a respect for her strength in the face of illness. He became weak, lost weight, and suffered from insomnia. As he had done many times before, Conan asked himself if he had done enough to help Touie. His mother assured him that he had done all that he could.

Gradually, however, Conan recovered his strength. In 1906 he again ran for a seat in the House of Commons. He was defeated for a second time, in another close election.

After a year of mourning Touie, Conan Doyle married Jean Leckie. The small wedding was at St. Margaret's Church in Westminster on September 18, 1907. "I married Miss Jean Leckie, the younger daughter of a Blackheath family whom I had known for years," Conan later wrote about his marriage. "The years have passed without one shadow coming to mar even for a moment the sunshine of my Indian summer which now deepens to a golden autumn. She and my three younger children . . . have made my home an ideally happy one."

Their new home was Doyle's country estate called

Conan loved his life at Windlesham, the home he shared with Jean.

Windlesham, which he had bought shortly before their marriage. He had it renovated and enlarged. The expense involved in remodeling was so great Conan joked that it should have been named "Swindlesham."

The new home was a gray shingled English Tudor mansion with a red tile roof. It had five rambling gables. Conan's study was beneath two of the gables. In an outer study sat his long-time secretary, Alfred Wood. There were many comforts within the new home: a billiard parlor, a baby grand piano, and extensive grounds and gardens. The Doyle family remained at Windlesham for the rest of Conan's life.

Despite the unhappy circumstances surrounding their falling in love, the marriage of Conan and Jean was happy. Jean shared many of Conan's interests. She was physically robust and healthy. They enjoyed a variety of sports, including tennis and rugby. Jean was an avid hunter and equestrian. Later in their life together, she also became a believer in Conan's spiritualist pursuits.

Conan and Jean's first child, a son they named Denis Percy Stewart Conan Doyle, was born in 1909. They would have two more children: another son, Adrian, in 1910, and Lena Jean, who was born in 1912.

Even living outside the large city in his tranquil country estate, Doyle remained very much in the public eye. It was only natural that the creator of the world's most famous fictional detective would become involved in some real-life crimes. He was also prompted by his concern for public affairs and his always active motivation to make sure that the "right thing was done." This knight errant impulse eventually led him to get involved in two murder cases.

Conan became intrigued with the first case after reading newspaper articles about the crime that his secretary clipped for his files in 1906. It involved a lawyer named George Edalji, who had been arrested in the Staffordshire village of Great Wyrley three years earlier for killing and mutilating farm animals. The son of an Indian born minister and an English mother, Edalji's academic skills had been honored with a Birmingham Law Society bronze medal. His father served as the vicar of the local parsonage.

Despite their achievements, the Edalji family suffered racial prejudice because of their Indian heritage. Pranks designed to embarrass the entire family occurred over a ten-year period. One of the most racially motivated of the town's citizens was also the chief constable, the town's top law enforcement official. He decided that George Edalji, the son, was responsible for the pranks pulled on the Edalji family. He also decided that George had committed the animal mutilations. The criminal acts were either the work of a diseased mind, or an effort of the younger Edalji to win the favor of his father, said the chief constable.

Although the constable had determined George Edalji's guilt, he had no evidence to support his opinion. He was determined to find some. When a pony was found mutilated on an August morning of 1903, the constable searched Edjali's room and, although he discovered no hard evidence implicating him, he arrested George for the mutilation. After a rushed trial that presented no real evidence of Edalji's guilt, the young man was found guilty and sentenced to seven years in prison. Mysteriously, three years later Edalji was sent home without any reason given for his early release.

After reading newspaper articles about Edalji's release, Conan made it his business to get George Edalji cleared of all the trumped-up charges. He wanted to clear the young man's record. "I realized that I was in the presence of an appalling tragedy, and that I was called upon to do what I could to set it right," he said.

Conan studied the transcripts of the trial, visited the scene of the crimes, and talked with family members. He pointed out that the maimings continued during Edalji's imprisonment and published a series of articles about Edalji in the *Daily Telegraph*, one of Great Britain's most popular newspapers. "England soon rang with the wrongs of George Edalji," Conan said triumphantly. "The wrongs would have been almost comic had they not had so tragic an upshot. If the whole land had been raked, I do not think that it would have been possible to find a man who was so unlikely, and indeed so incapable, of committing such actions." Many became indignant after learning what Edalji had suffered.

Conan's efforts were ultimately unsuccessful. Though he had been freed from prison, Edalji was still deemed to be a criminal and was not allowed to practice law. He was

Conan became convinced that George Edalji was mistreated because of racism.

also never compensated for the impact and cost the charges had on his life and career.

Conan later lamented in his memoirs, "It is a blot upon the record of English Justice, and even now it should be wiped out . . . What a travesty of Justice! . . . He [Edalji] came to my wedding reception, and there was no guest whom I was prouder to see."

Conan's courage in the Edalji affair was steady and clear-eyed. He received death threats because he was speaking out against racism. Though George Edalji never received a new trial, it became obvious to many in Great Britain that a miscarriage of justice had occurred. That led the British government to establish a Court of Appeals. Its purpose was to review the outcome of court cases and make sure that, in the future, defendants received a fair trial. The creation of this new court was due in large part to the persistence and detective work of Doyle.

Conan put his influence to use again for a very different kind of criminal. The Oscar Slater case differed in many ways. However, Slater, like Edalji, was the victim of prejudice. And the end result of all of his efforts would be more frustrating for Conan.

It took nineteen years before the Slater case was resolved. It began when Miss Marion Gilchrist, an elderly woman, was brutally murdered in her Glasgow, Scotland apartment in December 1908. Immediately after the murder, her maid, Helen Lambie, and a neighbor saw a young man hurrying from the scene. Some papers had been rifled through and a diamond brooch thought missing, but robbery was not the apparent motive.

Slater was a German Jew with a petty criminal record who had taken an assumed name. When he pawned a diamond brooch to pay for his passage to America, he was arrested and charged with murder. Then, Doyle said, "came the fiasco."

Evidence indicated that the brooch he pawned had been in Slater's possession for years and was clearly not Miss Gilchrist's. This, and the lack of any additional evidence against him, and the fact he could prove that he had been elsewhere when the crime had been committed should have won Slater's freedom. But it didn't. His real crime, Conan realized, was that Slater was luckless, "poor and friendless" with "bohemian" habits—he had lived with a woman out of wedlock—that shocked the Victorian Scots. Neither the police nor the public would relent and release Slater. He was forced to stand trial.

Slater was railroaded into a conviction and sentenced to death. Again, race played a major factor. The fact that he was Jewish seemed to be all the evidence most people needed to be convinced Slater was a murderer. Scaffolding was built for his execution. Conan was horrified by the travesty.

Doyle consulted with Sir Herbert Stephens, who also read the evidence, and declared publicly that there was no basis for the charges. There was not, he argued, even a "prima facie" case (which means "legally sufficient") against Slater. Once again, Conan undertook a newspaper campaign to appeal to the public. He also wrote a pamphlet about Slater's case and tried to win the government's sympathies for him.

Conan succeeded in winning some public sympathy. There was another examination of the case. But in Conan's opinion, the second examination was also an absolute farce. Slater's death sentence was lifted, but he remained imprisoned to serve a life sentence, although clearly he was an innocent man. It was "a dreadful blot upon the administration of justice in Scotland," Conan felt. "Somehow, somewhere, there comes a national punishment in return," he predicted. Despite Conan's best efforts, Slater remained in prison. The case would haunt Conan for years to come.

Other moral causes also attracted Doyle's attention. In 1908, Belgium annexed the Congo Free State. Soon, Conan had a "fresh task." He read accounts of the behavior of King Leopold II of Belgium and became concerned about Leopold's exploitation of the native people. Leopold siphoned off the ivory and rubber resources of the Congo while abusing the native population.

Ironically, the Belgians were behaving much as the British had in South Africa. In South Africa, natives had also been displaced and resources plundered and divided up among European powers. But, in Conan's view of things—which were always intensely patriotic—what was happening in the Congo was worse because Belgium, not the British Empire, was committing the atrocities.

The case of Oscar Slater occupied Conan for the last twenty years of his life.

For two years, Doyle wrote and called for reform in the Congo. Then he became convinced that reform was not enough. Belgium should walk away from her interests in Africa. He wrote a tract, "The Crime of the Congo," arguing his points. Like other endeavors, this one got the public's attention. Doyle refused to accept a penny of profit from its publication.

Conan's stands on these issues were often controversial. Rudyard Kipling wrote to his friend after "The Crime of the Congo" was published to warn that the Belgians might well tell Britain to mind its own business. Many others admired Doyle's efforts on behalf of the Congo. He was even invited to come to the United States and referee a boxing match between a black and white man. Conan was too immersed in his human rights campaign to go, but he regretted it.

Conan had always enjoyed his American adventures and relationships. His sphere of influence there continued to grow. He and the plainspoken President Theodore Roosevelt had met and personally corresponded. He chuckled that Roosevelt "was one of the raciest talkers I have ever met."

Conan began turning his attention to writing more stage plays. His drama about Sherlock Holmes ten years earlier had been a huge success. And in 1893 he had collaborated on a musical, *Jane Annie*, with J.M. Barrie, who later would write *Peter Pan*. Their collaboration had been panned by critics. Conan thought he and Barrie were "well abused" by the reviews, but sheepishly suggested they deserved it.

J.M. Barrie collaborated with Conan on several stage projects.

He had written the lyrics to the doomed production, admitting that the "result was not good."

Now Conan decided to write more for the theater. But he met with mixed success again. *In The House of Temperley* was found by most audiences, especially women, to be too violent. The next play, *Fires of Fate*, was produced during an unseasonably hot summer, and the plot demanded bright lights to simulate fire. The public didn't want to go and sit in hot theaters and swelter under the stage lights during a heat wave. Next, he launched another play, *Brigadier Gerard,* that was, by his own admission, only "mildly successful." However, in 1912, Conan agreed to dramatize his Sherlock Holmes tale, *The Speckled Band.* As always with the damned "calculating machine," the play based on the detective's adventures was a success. Truly, Conan was never going to escape the shadow cast by his least-loved creation.

Chapter Ten

The Great War

On April 10, 1912, the world was shocked when the luxury liner Titanic sank off the coast of Newfoundland. More than 1,500 passengers and crew drowned. Conan's nemesis, William Stead, was a Titanic victim.

George Bernard Shaw was completely outraged by the event. He felt that Britain had been too relaxed in its nautical regulations and safety standards for this new breed of huge luxury liners. He fired off criticism in the press.

Conan responded to Shaw, saying this was a time for mourning, not criticism. Shaw was contemptuous. In his opinion, the press had romanticized the Titanic disaster. The two writers dueled in the press with their pens.

About this time, Conan began to create a new fictional character. For the past six years, Sherlock Holmes had appeared in a few sporadic stories. But now, Doyle wanted a new character, one he could love as fervently as others had loved Holmes. He introduced the eclectic Professor Challenger in the fantasy, *The Lost World,* a story about a preserve of prehistoric creatures.

Doyle enjoyed the unruly, outrageous professor with the funny German accent so much that he started dressing up like him and trying to fool people with his impression. It delighted him to write about a clever man who had the sense of humor that Holmes lacked. Some of his friends believed that the professor was an uninhibited version of Conan himself.

He then wrote a sequel to *The Lost World* called *The Poison Belt*. But Professor Challenger never gained the public acceptance that Sherlock Holmes had enjoyed. His Professor Challenger books were read only by thousands, while Sherlock Holmes "had an audience of millions."

By 1912, another war was looming on the horizon for Britain and much of the world. Though people often called Conan Doyle a visionary, he had difficulty believing in the idea of a "German menace." He failed to accept that there was a serious war on the horizon. However, Queen Victoria was long dead and so was her grip on her grandson, Kaiser Wilhelm of Germany. The kaiser harbored deep and old personal resentments of the British.

Slowly, Conan became aware that Germany, seeking to extend its territory, was about to go to war with France, and that much of Europe soon would be involved, too.

Conan knew this coming war would be "the physical climax" of his life. It was to become a "fearsome whirlpool, where we all gyrated for four years, some sinking for ever, some washed up all twisted and bent."

Conan, as was becoming his standard action on great

public events, wrote a new tract entitled "England and the Next War" in 1913. Clearly, he argued, war lines and allies were being drawn. He proposed that England build a channel tunnel to import supplies in case its naval fleet was blockaded and couldn't import the necessary goods. He also prophesied that the use of submarines might bring Britain to its knees. He spelled out how it would happen in an imagined scenario he called "Danger!" and published in *The Strand*.

In the summer of 1914, Germany finally declared war on France and began invading the country. Germany also declared war against France's ally, Russia. German troops then invaded Switzerland, Luxembourg, and Belgium and soon were on the doorstep of Britain itself. By the end of the summer, England declared war on Germany.

Wartime London was wildly changed and charged. One never knew, Doyle said, what "evil bird" [airplane] flew overhead, or what "foul egg" [bomb] would be dropped." Windows were draped with curtains. Food was rationed, even at his Windlesham estate. Plays in London were staged with only candles for lights, as German zeppelins swooped above.

Conan was always challenged by war. His mind was preoccupied with defense maneuvers, and he sent proposals and ideas to the admiralty and Britain's military leaders. He developed the idea for a life-saving, inflatable vest to be used by sailors when a warship was attacked. He called it a "swimming collar." Next, he thought of inflatable lifeboats. Then he conceived the idea of an armored tank. Much later, he would make public appeals for helmets and body armor for soldiers, who were dying by the hundreds of thousands in trench warfare.

Doyle knew he was too old to serve as a soldier on the front lines, and he had been out of practice too long to become a battlefield doctor again. But he wanted to help.

He began by organizing a volunteer force called the Civilian Reserve. He notified Britain's War Office and began drills and training.

Private Sir Arthur Conan Doyle, now in his early fifties, was number 184343, fourth Volunteer Battalion Royal Sussex. His middle-aged charges rallied behind him. The Volunteer Battalion's ranks soon grew to 20,000. The War Office was displeased by Conan's initiatives and ordered the citizen's militia disbanded. But his reserves were quickly resurrected by wiser men. Many of their ranks were in their fifties and sixties, but were undeterred by their age. They marched as much as fourteen miles a day in training. Conan was determined to be a central part of the war.

His son Kingsley was sent to the front lines along with his wife's brother Malcolm. Kingsley had a different temperament than his father. He hated war. Conan himself tried to get moved to the front lines, too. Even his private secretary was now in active service and held the title of Major Wood. Wood was sent to the front lines alongside others whom Conan held dear.

Conan found the War Office to be a source of continual

Conan (second from the right) near the western front during World War I.

irritation and hindrance to his ideas. No matter. He was immersed in the military and he'd find a way. Conan was a man who had access to the powerful, and that often worked toward his advantage. Eventually, it got him to the front lines where he wanted to be.

Conan was recruited by the Foreign Office to spend time in Italy and France writing as a special wartime correspondent for *The Daily Chronicle,* an English newspaper. His press pass allowed him to go behind British lines, moving among the troops wearing his old deputy lieutenant's uniform from his volunteer militia unit. He even found his old secretary, Major Wood, in the French town of Beauquesne and inspected his work. The writer brooded through the deadened and darkened streets of Paris.

Next, Conan spent time observing Italian soldiers. While in Italy, he had what he called a psychic experience. Two names reverberated in his head when he woke from a dream. He recorded the experience and had people witness it and sign the paper as proof. Later, the names turned out to be significant to the war: one was a war front locale, the other a ship on which he eventually sailed to Australia. This was an experience beyond "all possible coincidence," he said. He was convinced the subconscious mind was affected by information from the spirits of the dead.

In 1917, a wartime trawler was commissioned with Doyle's name. After it was sunk by a submarine, he was given the ship's bell as a memento.

It had been almost four years since Doyle had written his last Holmes story, "The Adventure of the Dying Detective." The war had taken up so much of his time. But in 1917 he managed to write a short piece, "The Last Bow: The War Service of Sherlock Holmes."

Eventually, the "evil bird" of war swooped down on the Doyle household. The first member of the family to die in the service of war was his brother-in-law, Malcolm Leckie, who had recently served in the medical service along with Conan's son Kingsley. Then his wife's best friend, Lily Loder-Symonds, died of natural causes after losing her three brothers in battle. Conan also lost two of his nephews to the war. Next, his brother-in-law, Major Leslie Oldham, was killed in battle.

On October 28, 1918 Kingsley, Conan's eldest child,

died after suffering battle wounds. Conan was inconsolable. He wrote that Kingsley was "one of the grandest boys in body and soul that ever a father was blessed with."

Armistice Day, the end of the war, followed only two weeks after Kingsley's death. But the fatalities didn't stop. As in all wars, disease carried off more soldiers than battle. Conan's brother Innes, only forty and an adjutant general, died of pneumonia. He had been worn out by the war. "I am a soldier," were his deathbed words. He left a tiny son, John, living at Windlesham, who was now fatherless.

Apart from his wife, there were few Conan could turn to as he summed up war's toll on his personal life. All around him the world had changed. Life at Windlesham had been upended with so many deaths, and he was faced with a profound crisis of the spirit. What did all this suffering mean? Was there no way to find a solution to the terrible misery that was often human life?

Chapter Eleven

Last Years

World War I exacted a heavy price from Doyle. Great Britain, and the rest of Europe, had lost an entire generation of young men in battle. Conan had lost his son and brother. For the first time in his life, including the darkest days of Touie's illness, Conan felt despair. Life seemed to be so futile and cruel. Why were we born only to suffer? For a period of time, he could see no way out. Maybe Sherlock Holmes could solve all problems by using his wits and applying science to unsolved mysteries. But real life didn't work that way.

As a young man Conan had rejected Catholicism. While his mother had convinced him to have his children baptized, he professed no belief in any religion for decades. Now he was forced to reconsider some of the ultimate questions. Was there life beyond death? Did the spirit endure? He needed answers, and only in moving beyond the boundaries of rational thinking could he find them.

Conan had maintained an interest in spiritualism since General Drayson had introduced him to it four decades earlier. Now he set about another systematic study. This time, however, he was motivated more by emotional pain than by his intellectual curiosity. As he approached the last years of his life, he wanted answers to the ultimate question: What happened to our spirit after the body died? The answers he eventually arrived at indicated how much Arthur Conan Doyle was a man of his era.

Spiritualism, the belief that the spirit and personality continues beyond death, and that the living can communicate with the dead through "mediums," was highly popular in the early twentieth century. Many famous and not-so-famous people voiced a belief in the abilities of mediums to communicate with the dead. Spiritualism also advocated that each individual take responsibility for his or her own actions in order to progress as a soul. It denied the existence of hell, and instead viewed the earth as a "training-ground" for the spirit.

Spiritualism was controversial. Most organized religions dismissed it as being run by charlatans, people who used tricks and fakery, to convince their followers that they could communicate with the dead. Nevertheless, it was a movement growing more and more popular in Britain.

Doyle had been exploring spiritualism ever since he began investigating psychic phenomenon at General Drayson's request when he was still a young man. He was a slow convert. The more rational, logical side of his nature kept posing nagging questions. Why, for example, did the spirits of the dead return and then only perform such trivial acts as knocking on a wall? It seemed to the younger man that a spirit would have more important things to do. He remained skeptical while pondering such questions as these. His skepticism was altered by the tragedies brought about by the war. He now had a more powerful need to believe that there was life after death, and that it was possible for the dead to communicate with the loved ones left behind.

Conan was not alone. Psychic phenomenon was stirring the interest of many intellectuals of his time. American philosopher and psychologist William James and other respected public figures either believed in spiritualism or refused to totally reject the possibility of making contact with the dead. Nevertheless, it shocked many people when the creator of Sherlock Holmes became a public advocate of mediums and seances.

During the war, in 1915, Conan had declared publicly that he was a believer in spiritualism. By 1917, he was touring and giving public lectures on the topic. Eventually, he traveled to Australia, France, and the United States pressing its case. He detailed his tours in his writing, *Wanderings of a Spiritualist,* published in 1921.

During the decade of the 1920s Conan logged fifty thousand miles and spoke to nearly 250,000 people as an advocate of spiritualism. He refused to accept pay for his engagements, receiving only expenses. Profits from his talks were contributed to reprintings. Jean was also a believer. She gave demonstrations of automatic writing, and Doyle would lecture afterward.

Many of his readers began wondering how the creator of a fictional character who so steadfastly maintained faith in science could believe in spiritualism and psychic phenomenon. Conan was often ridiculed, but he continued advocating his beliefs. He said publicly that he was not afraid to venture outside the normal religious beliefs.

Spiritualism was soon absorbing all of Conan's life. He published a book entitled *The New Revelation.* It was swiftly followed by *The Vital Message.* Both books sought to prove that psychic phenomenon was a reality. It was, some described, as if an "imperative duty had been laid on him, a humanitarian duty. The world was now at peace, sitting at a ruined hearth."

Conan revisited South Africa, twenty-eight years after his Boer War campaign. He toured from Cape Town to Johannesburg, calling on famous psychics and spiritualists. He concerned himself with the ghosts of the dead and talked freely and openly on the subject there.

Though spiritualism took up most of his time, Conan remained involved in other book projects. For several years, he had been writing a history of Britain's involvement in World War I. He finished it in 1920 and saw it published in six volumes.

Conan's most famous public controversy over spiritualism was retold in a 1997 movie entitled *Fairy Tale.* He wrote a book and spoke publicly about two young sisters who had photographed what they claimed were fairies and elves. When the photos were published they became the talk of all England. In Doyle's book about the girls, *The Coming of the Fairies,* he said he was convinced there was overwhelming evidence that little fairies actually existed. This brought great derision onto the head of the once highly respected writer. He became the butt of jokes.

Doyle brushed aside his critics and continued writing on spiritualism. During the war, he started his memoirs, and he continued with the project when the war ended. In 1923, his memoirs were serialized in *The Strand.*

Conan turned again to fiction, but with a spiritual twist. In 1924, Professor Challenger became a convert to spiritualism in *The Land of the Mists.* (The book was originally entitled, *The Psychic Adventures of Edward Malone.*) This alienated some of his readers. Doyle, however, did not try the experiment with his most popular character. Sherlock Holmes remained the pure scientist to the end, in the stories collected under the title *The Case Book of Sherlock Holmes.* Conan never tampered with his beliefs.

By now, Conan whole-heartedly accepted the existence of fairies, spirit photographs, kinetic energy, levitation, and other psychic phenomena. He also investigated house hauntings and other psychic events. He believed that the human body could disintegrate, atom by atom, and be reconstructed on another site. He busied himself studying the automatic writings that said to be the spirit works of great writers such as Charles Dickens and Conan's old acquaintance, Oscar Wilde.

Publicly embracing spiritualism cost Conan the respect and

Conan in 1930, the last year of his life.

support of many who had admired him. The famous magician Harry Houdini scoffed at Conan's conversion. Houdini believed his long-time friend had been "hoodwinked" by fraudulent displays of psychic phenomenon.

Conan's pronouncements on spiritualism were a rude shock to those who had so admired the writer and patriot. He received outraged letters, some even addressing him as evil. But he doggedly tended the seeds, he wrote in his memoirs, that would survive the "cold blasts of a hostile world."

Though spiritualism took up most of his time, Conan remained haunted by the old Oscar Slater case from years earlier. Slater was still in prison for the 1908 murder of an elderly woman. In 1925, Doyle again resolved to help him. He convinced a friend and journalist to write another book about the case, *The Truth About Oscar Slater*. This second effort for justice finally earned some results. Slater was finally pardoned in 1927.

1927 was the same year that Doyle published what would be his last Sherlock Holmes story. It was called "The Adventure of Shoscombe Old Place."

By the end of the 1920s, Conan was nearing seventy and was ill with heart disease. He continued traveling and speaking on the subject that consumed most of his last years—spiritualism. In 1929 he visited Sweden, Norway, and Denmark. When he returned to London he was gasping for breath and doctors warned him that he could die if he continued his lectures and travels.

The warning didn't deter Conan. Within days, he was speaking at the famed Albert Hall in London, though he was unsteady on his feet.

Conan's health began to deteriorate even more. He began spending most of his time back at Windlesham, the family estate. By the summer of 1930 he spent his days in his study, writing and answering letters from friends. He never stopped working, even when he had to be given oxygen to help him breathe.

Conan made a last trip to London to speak, though his doctors begged him not to go. He grew weaker.

On the early morning of July 7, 1930, Doyle was helped out of bed to sit in a chair looking out the window. He knew the end was near and refused to die in bed. Then, with his wife and children gathered about him, he closed his eyes and slipped away. He was seventy-one.

Conan was buried with a modest headstone reading "Steel True, Blade Straight" near a garden shed on the grounds of Windlesham. A special train was needed to bring in all the flowers from friends and fans around the world.

A memorial service was held with a medium named Estelle Roberts presiding. An empty chair was placed between the widow Lady Jean Doyle and her children. The empty chair was for Sir Arthur Conan Doyle.

The Doyle family was certain they experienced his presence that day in the chair. Later that month, Lady Doyle confirmed this and other "evidence" of his posthumous materializations in an interview with the *London Daily Herald.*

Today, while his spiritualists beliefs are no longer in favor, few doubt that Sir Arthur Conan Doyle had been ahead of his time as a writer of mystery and adventure stories. His literary inventions, Sherlock Holmes and John Watson, molded the modern detective novel. Only the American tough-guy private eye can hope to rival the image of Holmes with his magnifying glass and deer stalker hat as the most recognizable character in all crime literature. There have been few mystery writers since Holmes was first created who were not influenced in some way by Conan Doyle's mystery stories and novels. *The Hound of the Baskervilles* is probably the most famous detective novel ever written.

In real life, Sir Arthur Conan Doyle influenced the world. He uncovered a range of innovations, inventions, and discoveries. He convinced the British judiciary to develop a court of appeals. He pushed the British army to adapt certain evasive strategies, such as the wearing of metal helmets for the first time, and to use lifeboats and life rafts. He advocated a wider application of armored tanks in battle. He suggested a channel tunnel (or chunnel) connecting Great Britain to mainland Europe a hundred years before it was undertaken.

Through Sherlock Holmes, Conan Doyle taught scientific skills later adopted by the police worldwide. Those included the analysis of dust for clues, the differentiation of tobacco ashes, and the use of plaster casts in forensics and detection.

Sherlock Holmes was as real to his readers as was Conan Doyle the writer. In his heyday, Sherlock Holmes received almost as much December mail (addressed to his fictitious Baker Street address in London) as Santa Claus. Thousands of tourists were as interested in seeing Baker Street as they were in visiting Buckingham Palace. Even a London trolley line was named for him . . . and ships . . . and countless children.

Doyle's good friend Rudyard Kipling advised in his famous poem that a man should "Walk with kings, yet keep the common touch." Doyle did exactly that. He remembered his humble beginnings. Though he was entertained by royalty, sultans, prime ministers, viceroys, kaisers, and presidents. He championed the underdog and fought for the ordinary man. Just like the knights he admired, he was a righter of wrongs. Sir Arthur Conan Doyle lived up to the knighthood he was given by a king. He was a big man, and he lived a big life.

Major Works

Novels
Micah Clarke, 1887
A Study in Scarlet, 1887
The Sign of Four, 1890
The White Company, 1890
The Refugees, 1891
The Great Shadow, 1892
The Stark Munro Letters, 1895
The Exploits of Brigadier Gerard, 1896
The Hound of the Baskervilles, 1902
Adventures of Gerard, 1903
The Lost World, 1912
The Valley of Fear, 1915
The Land of Mists, 1926

Short Story Collections
The Adventures of Sherlock Holmes, 1892
The Memoirs of Sherlock Holmes, 1893
The Return of Sherlock Holmes, 1905
The Last Bow, 1917
The Case Book of Sherlock Holmes, 1927

Nonfiction
The Great Boer War, 1900
The War in South Africa—Its Cause and Conduct, 1902
The Story of Mr. George Edalji, 1907
The Crime of the Congo, 1909
The Case of Oscar Slater, 1912
Great Britian and the Next War, 1914
The History of Spiritualism, 1926
The Edge of the Unknown, 1930

Bibliography

Carr, John Dickinson. *The Life of Sir Arthur Conan Doyle.* 1949. New York: Harper and Brothers.

Cox, Don Richard. *Arthur Conan Doyle.* 1985. New York: Frederick Ungar Publishing Co.

Doyle, Sir. Arthur Conan. *The Complete Sherlock Holmes.* 1930. New York: Doubleday and Co.

Doyle, Sir. Arthur Conan. *The Lost World.* 1920. New York: Random House.

Doyle, Sir Arthur Conan. *Memories and Adventures.* 1924. Boston: Little, Brown and Company.

Green, Richard Lancelyn, Ed. *The Sherlock Holmes Letters.* 1986. Iowa City: University of Iowa Press.

Higham, Charles. *The Adventures of Conan Doyle: The Life of the Creator of Sherlock Holmes.* 1976. New York: W.W. Norton and Company.

Hoehling, Mary. *The Real Sherlock Holmes.* 1965. New York: Julian Messner, Inc.

Jaffe, Jacqueline A. *Arthur Conan Doyle.* 1987. Boston: Twayne Publishers.

Keating, H.R.F. *Sherlock Holmes: The Man and His World.* 1979. New York: Charles Scribner's Sons.

Nordon, Pierre. *Conan Doyle: A Biography.* 1967. New York: Holt, Rinehart and Winston, Inc.

Orel, Harold. *Sir Arthur Conan Doyle: Interviews and Recollections.* 1991. New York: St. Martin's Press.

Panati, Charles. *Panati's Extraordinary Endings of Practically Everything and Everybody.* 1989. New York: Harper & Row, Publishers.

Shreffler, Philip A., Ed. *The Baker Street Reader.* 1984. Westport: Greenwood Press.

Wood, James Playsted. *The Man Who Hated Sherlock Holmes: A Life of Sir Arthur Conan Doyle.* 1965. New York: Pantheon Books.

Index